What this book is all about . . . . .

This picture dictionary lists a lot of words and explains what they mean. The pictures will help you to understand the words.

At the end of every chapter there is a puzzle picture. Look at these pictures and see if you can remember the names you have seen in the pages.

You will learn about lots of new words and find out that learning to read can be fun!

ISBN 0-86163-128-5 (cased)
ISBN 0-86163-082-3 (paperbound)

Copyright © Thomas Nelson and Sons Ltd

First published by Award Publications 1983
Reprinted 1988

Published by Award Publications Limited,
Spring House, Spring Place,
Kentish Town, London NW5 3BH

Printed in Hungary

abcdefghijklmnopqrstuvwxyz

PICTURE DICTIONARY

A	B	C	D	E	F	G
H	I	J	K	L	M	N
O	P	Q	R	S	T	U
V	W	X	Y	Z		

ILLUSTRATED BY DAVID NOCKELS

DESIGNED BY DESMOND MARWOOD AND PREPARED IN CONSULTATION WITH

Dr. Elizabeth Goodacre, B.Sc., Ph.D.

AWARD PUBLICATIONS — LONDON

abcdefghijklmnopqrstuvwxyz

a

a	b	c	d	e	f	g	h	i	j	k	l	m	n	o	p	q	r	s	t	u	v	w	x	y
A	B	C	D	E	F	G	H	I	J	K	L	M	N	O	P	Q	R	S	T	U	V	W	X	Y

above

Above these words is a picture of two birds. The blue bird is above the black bird. It is higher up in the sky.

absent

Tim is away from school. He is absent from school because he is ill. The teacher will mark him absent until he returns.

acorn

The acorn is a nut.
Acorns grow on oak trees and you see them in Autumn.

add

To add is to put together.
If you add two and six does it make eight?

address

The address is on the letter. It tells the postman where to take the letter. This letter is addressed to Jane Brown.

adult

Grown up. This is a little boy. His daddy is an adult.

adventure

When something exciting happens. Explorers and spacemen have adventures. Tom had an adventure when he went fishing.

aeroplane

Aeroplanes fly in the sky. This aeroplane is landing. What colour is this aeroplane?

after

Tim goes to bed after eating his supper. His dog goes after him up the stairs.

A a

again.

 The ball is down on the ground.

The ball is up in the air.  Now it is up in the air again

ajar.

The door is closed.

The door is open.

Now it is open just a bit and so it is ajar

alligator

This is an alligator. Alligators swim in the water. What big mouths they've got!

almost

It is almost nine o'clock It is now nine o'clock  Tim is yawning and is almost ready to go to bed.

ambulance

The ambulance is going to the hospital. It has a red cross on it.

angry

When we get cross we feel angry.
The boy is angry with his friend.

ankle

The ankle is part of your body.
It is between your foot and your
leg. This girl has hurt her ankle.

animal

An animal is a living thing that
moves and feels. Horses, fish,
birds, bees and snakes are all
animals. Do you know the
names of any other animals?

another

One more. The boy has had a
drink and now he is asking
for another.

A a

answer

When you add two and six the answer is eight. This is the right answer to the sum.

any

Some out of a lot. Is there any cake for Tim?

apple

Apples grow on trees.
The pig likes to eat an apple.

April

The fourth month of the year. We get showers in the month of April.

apron

Mummy wears an apron.
The apron covers her dress and
keeps it clean.

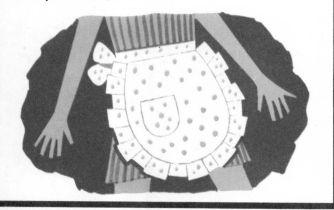

archer

The archer uses a bow and
arrow. Will the archer hit the
apple on the boy's head?

ark

An ark is a sort of boat.
Noah built an ark and all
the animals went in two by two.

arm

The part of a person's body
between the shoulder and the
hand. She has a bracelet on her arm

arrow

The archer has shot the arrow
from his bow. The arrow hits
the apple.

A a

artist

The artist paints a picture.
What colour will the artist
paint the horse?

asleep

Tim was almost asleep.
Is he asleep now?

August

August is the eighth month of
the year. It is often hot in August
and people go to the seaside on holiday.

axe

An axe is a
very sharp tool.

axle

The axle is the bar on which
a wheel turns. This wheel has
come off its axle

Now see if you can spot all the things in this picture beginning with the letter a and match them with their names at the bottom of the page.

These are the things beginning with the letter a.

axe	artist	alligator	acorn
arrow	apple	apron	aeroplane

b

a	b	c	d	e	f	g	h	i	j	k	l	m	n	o	p	q	r	s	t	u	v	w	x	y
A	B	C	D	E	F	G	H	I	J	K	L	M	N	O	P	Q	R	S	T	U	V	W	X	Y

back

Part of a person or thing. The girl fell off the back of her bicycle. She hurt her back.

bacon

It is the meat of the pig. We cook bacon and often make a meal of bacon and eggs.

badge

He put the Sheriff's badge on his shirt. Now everyone knows Bill is Sheriff of Little Creek.

bake

Mummy has put a cake in the oven to bake. A baker bakes bread in his oven and then he sells it.

bald

This man has hair on his head.

This man does not have hair on his head. He is bald.

bark

The Indian strips the bark from the outside of the tree.

It is also the sound made by a dog. The policeman's dog barks.

barrow

Tim has put some apples in his barrow. It can be pushed.

basket

Mother takes a basket when she goes to the shops. She puts all the things she buys into it.

battle

A fight. This battle is between the cowboys and Indians. The battle started when the Indians attacked.

B b

beach

A beach is the almost flat sandy part beside the sea. It can be little stones or shingle.

beat

To beat something is to hit it again and again! Tim is beating his big drum.

because

Tim is running to school because he is late. He is late because he did not get up when Mummy called him.

beef

It is the meat of an ox, cow or bull. Mummy is cooking some beef stew.

before

Tim had his supper before he went to bed. He went upstairs before his dog.

16

begin

The ice cream begins to melt.
These pages are near the
beginning of the book.

bend

A curve. Can you
see the bend in
the bow?

berry

A berry is a small
juicy fruit with seeds
instead of a stone. Do
you like blackberries?

between

The Indian is
between two trees.

behind

The Indian is behind the tree.
The cowboy is behind the Indian.

best

The first cake tastes
good. The second cake
tastes better but the
third is best.

blind

A blind is a cover
for a window.
A person is blind
when they cannot see.

B b

both

When you are talking about two things. Both boys had two apples each. Tim ate one but John ate both of his.

bow

The archer uses a bow to shoot his arrows. He pulls the string on his bow and then lets go of the arrow.

brick

A brick is a block of baked clay. Houses are built with bricks. Toy bricks are made of wood or plastic.

build

When we make something. This man is going to build a house. It will be a fine building.

ow see if you can spot all the things in this
icture beginning with the letter b and match
hem with their names at the bottom of the page.

hese are the things beginning with the letter b.

barrow	bacon	berry	blind
basket	badge	brick	

C

a	b	c	d	e	f	g	h	i	j	k	l	m	n	o	p	q	r	s	t	u	v	w	x	y
A	B	C	D	E	F	G	H	I	J	K	L	M	N	O	P	Q	R	S	T	U	V	W	X	Y

cabbage

A cabbage is a vegetable. We have a cabbage with our beef stew. Do you like cabbage?

cake

There is a big cake on this plate. Tim takes a piece of cake with the cherry on top.

camera

A camera takes photographs. Tim's Daddy is taking a photograph of him with a camera. It will be a good picture.

captain

This man is a captain. He is in charge of a ship. There are also captains in the army. Jim is captain of his team. He is leader.

car

Here are some cars. Each car has an engine inside it to make it move. Which motor car would you like to drive?

caravan

A caravan is a house on wheels.
This caravan is being pulled by a
car. At night the people in the
car will sleep in the caravan.

carrot

A carrot is
another vegetable.
Rabbits like to
eat carrots.

castle

A castle is
a strong building.
It was built
in the old days.

chair

Tim is sitting
in a chair. What
colour is the
chair?

careless

Jim was careless. He was
clumsy and did not look
what he was doing.
He must be more careful.

cat

A cat is a small
animal. Have you
a cat as a pet? Big
cats are in zoos.

children

Children are
boys and girls.
Tom is a child.

21

C c

chocolate

Chocolate is a sweet. Tim and John are eating a bar of chocolate. They also like boxes of chocolates and chocolate ice-creams.

choose

To choose means to pick out. Jack hopes the captain will choose him for the team.

Christmas

Christmas Day is on 25th December. It is the birthday of Jesus Christ.

Church

A church is a large, tall building. It is a place where people go to think about God and Jesus. Is there a church near your home?

city

A city is a big town. There are lots of offices in cities and some people live there, too. London is a city.

clock

A clock is a machine that measures the time.

clothes

Clothes are all the things we wear. The clothes that Jane wears are a jumper and skirt, a coat, a hat, shoes and socks.

coat

Tim puts on his coat before he goes out. It will help to keep him warm. Tim's dog has a thick coat.

colour

This artist is using a lot of colours. Red, yellow, blue are the names of colours. Can you think of another colour?

cost

The cost is how much we pay for a thing. How much did this book cost?

£2.50

50p

C c

count

We count things when we want to find out how many there are. Can you count the sweets?

cow

A cow is an animal. You can see cows in fields in the country.

Cows give us our milk.

crowd

A crowd is a lot of people or things. The platform is very crowded with people.

crumb

A crumb is a very small piece of something. Can you see the crumbs on the plate? Mummy puts the crumbs out for the birds to eat.

customer

Tim is buying some chocolate at the shop. He is a customer.

ow see if you can spot all the things in this
icture beginning with the letter c and match
hem with their names at the bottom of the page.

hese are the things beginning with the letter c.

| cabbage | cat | clock | carrot |
| cake | car | cow | castle |

d

a	b	c	d	e	f	g	h	i	j	k	l	m	n	o	p	q	r	s	t	u	v	w	x	y
A	B	C	D	E	F	G	H	I	J	K	L	M	N	O	P	Q	R	S	T	U	V	W	X	Y

dance

To dance is to move about to music. Jane and her friends are dancing.

danger

We are in danger when something may harm us. It is dangerous to run across roads without looking.

dark

It is dark when there is no light. Some children take a light to bed.

December

December is the twelfth and last month of the year. Christmas Day is the 25th December.

decorate

To make something more beautiful. Mum decorated the room for Sam's birthday party. The decorations are grand.

deep

Deep means far down. The roadmen are digging a deep hole. It goes down deep.

diamond

A diamond is a precious stone. It is valuable and can cost a lot.

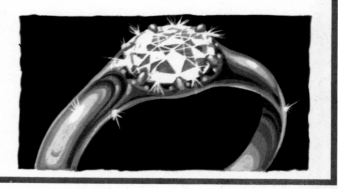

dictionary

This book is a dictionary. It lists a lot of words and explains them.

different

Things are different when they are not alike. An apple and a pear are both fruit. They are not the same. They are different shapes.

dinosaur

Dinosaurs were large reptiles that used to live on earth.

do

We use lots of do "words. Do stop shouting. Don't make a noise.

does
did
doing
done

D d

doctor

A doctor is a person who knows how to care for people who are sick or hurt. He tries to make them better.

dog

A dog is an animal. Some people keep dogs as pets. Some dogs can help people.

doll

A doll is a toy. There are many sorts of dolls.

door

Rooms and cupboards have doors. They are a way of keeping things out. Tom forgot to shut the door.

double

Double means to make twice as much. If you add the same again, you double it. If you add two and two you have four.

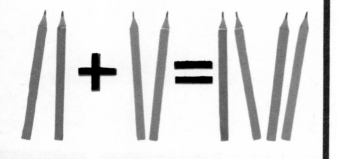

dozen

A dozen is twelve. Here are a dozen jelly babies.

draw

When we draw we make a picture with a pencil or pen.

drawbridge

A drawbridge is a bridge that can be lifted.

down

The boy is going up. The girl is coming down. She came downstairs for her doll.

dream

When Tim was asleep he had a dream. He was dreaming.

dry

This boy's hands are wet. He is using a towel to dry them.

29

D d

duck

A duck is a bird that swims and flies. Baby ducks are called ducklings.

dump

A dump is a place where we put the things we do not want. The dustmen are dumping the rubbish.

dungeon

A dungeon is a room deep under the ground. In castles prisoners could be kept in the dungeon. A dungeon needed to have a very strong door.

dustbin

We put rubbish in the dustbin. Mother empties the dustpan. The dustmen will empty it into the dustcart.

Now see if you can spot all the things in this
picture beginning with the letter d and match
them with their names at the bottom of the page.

These are the things beginning with the letter d.

| diamond | doctor | doll | dustbin |
| dictionary | duck | door | dinosaur |

e

a	b	c	d	e	f	g	h	i	j	k	l	m	n	o	p	q	r	s	t	u	v	w	x	y
A	B	C	D	E	F	G	H	I	J	K	L	M	N	O	P	Q	R	S	T	U	V	W	X	Y

each

Each doll has a pretty dress. There are buttons on each dress.

ear

People and animals hear with their ears. The ear is also a part of some plants with the grain inside it.

early

Tim has arrived at school at ten minutes to nine. Lessons do not start until nine o'clock. He is ten minutes early.

east

The sun rises in the east. This aeroplane is flying to the east.

Easter

Easter is an important time for people who go to church. On Easter Sunday people have Easter eggs.

easy

A thing is easy when it is not hard to do. These girls are skipping. It is easy for them.

eat

We eat when we chew and swallow food. Will Tom be able to eat all these Easter eggs?

edge

The glass is near the edge. It is not near the middle. It may be knocked off.

A knife has an edge.

egg

Baby birds come out of eggs. Chickens, snakes and alligators come out of eggs.

E e

eight

Eight is a number. If you add ten to eight you get eighteen. Eight times ten is eighty.

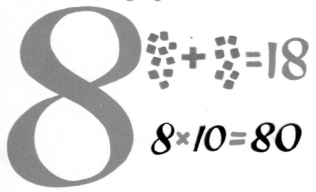

elbow

Your elbow is part of your arm. This boy is resting his elbows on the desk.

elephant

This is an elephant. It uses its long trunk to pick up food and water.

eleven

Eleven is the number which comes after ten. There are eleven players in a football team.

emerald

An emerald is another precious stone. There is an emerald in this ring.

34

empty

The nest is empty.
The birds have gone.

end

The end is the last part of something. Sally's friends are holding the ends of the rope for her.

Z is the last letter.
It is at the end of this book.

engine

An engine is a machine that pulls or pushes things to make them move.

enough

We have enough when we have as much as we want.

entrance

When we go into a building we go through the entrance. This is the entrance to the school.

equal

Equal is the same in size, amount or number. The liquid in the fat glass is equal to the liquid in the tall glass.

E e

Eskimo

Here is an Eskimo.
Where he lives he has to build
his house of packed snow.

every

The sun comes up every day.
Tom can spell some other
"every" words.

excite

When we excite someone we stir
up their feelings. The boys were
excited when their team
scored a goal.

explorer

An explorer is a person who
travels in little known places.
He finds out about them.

eye

We all have two eyes. People and
animals see with their eyes.

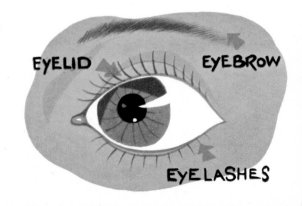

Now see if you can spot all the things in this picture beginning with the letter e and match them with their names at the bottom of the page.

These are the things beginning with the letter e.

ear	elephant	eye	explorer
egg	entrance	Eskimo	emerald

f

a	b	c	d	e	f	g	h	i	j	k	l	m	n	o	p	q	r	s	t	u	v	w	x	y	z
A	B	C	D	E	F	G	H	I	J	K	L	M	N	O	P	Q	R	S	T	U	V	W	X	Y	Z

face

Your face is the front part of your head. Your eyes, nose and mouth are all parts of your face. Freddy is washing his face.

factory

A factory is a building where things are made. Cars are being made in this factory.

family

A family is made up of parents and their children.

DAUGHTER SON MOTHER FATHER GRANDMOTHER GRANDFATHER

famous

Famous means very well known. Here are some famous things.

Henry VIII

fast

The car is travelling very fast. It goes faster than the bicycle. The aeroplane is the fastest.

fat

Here are two clowns. One is fat and one is thin.

February

February is the second month of the year. It is often cold in February.

fence

A fence can keep things in or out. Also, using a sword is called fencing.

field

A field is a piece of land. It can have a hedge or a wall or a fence around it.

feather

Feathers grow on birds. There are all sorts of different feathers. Which feathers do you like best?

few

Few means when there are not a lot. This bird has few feathers.

finger

Part of your hand. You have four fingers and one thumb on each hand.

thumb

F f

fire

Here is a fire. Fire gives us heat and light. It can be a friend but it can also be dangerous.

first

Tim is first in the race. He is ahead of all the other boys. He will get the first prize.

fish

Fish live in the water. Here are some different types of fish.

five

Five is a number. We have five toes on each foot. If you add ten to five you get fifteen. Five times ten is fifty.

40

flag

This flag is called the Union Jack. It is the flag of Great Britain. Each country has its own flag.

floor

Rooms have floors and walls and ceilings. We stand on the floor. The ceiling is above us.

food

Food is all the things we eat. Fruit, eggs, meat, vegetables and fish are all food. What is your favourite food?

fork

We use a knife and fork to eat our meals. We hold our food steady with the fork while we cut it up with the knife.

41

F f

four

Four is a number.
So are fourteen and forty.

freeze

To freeze is to turn into ice.
When water on the pond freezes
it turns into ice. The birds cannot
get a drink. The water is frozen.

front

The front is the
part that faces
forward. The driver
is at the front.

fruit

There are many sorts of fruit.
Which is your favourite fruit?

full

When something is full there is
no more room in it. The glass is
full of orange juice.

Now see if you can spot all the things in this picture beginning with the letter f and match them with their names at the bottom of the page.

These are the things beginning with the letter f.

| face | feather | fish | fork |
| factory | flag | fire | fence |

g

a	b	c	d	e	f	g	h	i	j	k	l	m	n	o	p	q	r	s	t	u	v	w	x	y
A	B	C	D	E	F	G	H	I	J	K	L	M	N	O	P	Q	R	S	T	U	V	W	X	Y

game

When we play we usually play a game. Football, hide-and-seek and dominoes are all games. What games do you play?

garage

A garage is a building where cars are kept. There is a car in this garage next to the house.

garden

A garden is a place where flowers, fruit or vegetables are grown. Daddy looks after the garden. He is a gardener.

gas

Gas is used for heating and cooking. Mummy cooks food on the gas stove. Have you got any gas fires in your house?

gate

A gate is a sort of door in a fence or wall. It can be open or shut.

giraffe

A giraffe is an animal with a very long neck and long legs. Giraffes come from Africa. You can see a giraffe in a zoo. This one is called George.

gift

When you give something to someone it is a gift. Jane's gift to her mother is a box of chocolates.

giant

A giant is a very big man. There are very many fairy stories about giants.

glove

We wear gloves on our hands. They keep our hands dry, or warm or clean.

Washing up gloves

Fur gloves

Gardening gloves

go

When we go we move from one place to another. Tim and his friends go to school on their bicycles.

G g

gold

Watches, rings and other jewellery are sometimes made of gold. Gold is a bright yellow metal. It is very valuable.

grey

Grey is also a colour. If you mix black with white you get grey.

guard

To guard something is to take care of it.
The dog guards the house.

green

Green is a colour.
All these things are green.

grow

When we grow, we get bigger.
Tim grew six inches last year.

Now see if you can spot all the things in this picture beginning with the letter g and match them with their names at the bottom of the page.

These are the things beginning with the letter g.

giraffe	glove	gold	garage
gate	gift	guard	giant

h

a	b	c	d	e	f	g	h	i	j	k	l	m	n	o	p	q	r	s	t	u	v	w	x	y
A	B	C	D	E	F	G	H	I	J	K	L	M	N	O	P	Q	R	S	T	U	V	W	X	Y

hair

Hair grows on your head. It can be fair or dark. If it grows on your face it can be a beard or a moustache.

A dog has hair on its body.

handle

The handle is the part which can be held. A suitcase has a handle. Pans have handles.

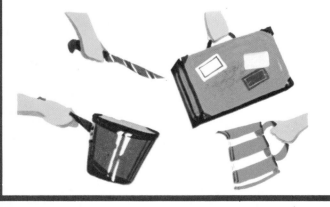

half

A half is one of two equal parts. Mummy has cut the apple into two halves. She is giving one half to Harry and the other half to John.

handkerchief

A handkerchief is a square of material. We keep our handkerchiefs in our pockets. Bob is wiping his nose with his handkerchief.

hard

Hard means firm.
Steel is hard.
A pillow is soft.
Hard can also mean difficult.

hat

A hat is a covering for the head.
There are all sorts of hats.
Some hats are called caps.

jockey's cap | school cap | top hat | sun bonnet | woman's hat

hay

Hay is grass which has been cut
and dried. Hay is used as food
for cattle and horses.

heat

Heat is warmth.
Jane is warming
her hands by the
heat of the fire.

John is warming
himself in the
heat from the sun.

heavy

This roller is heavy. Harry finds it
difficult to pull up the steps.
Because it is heavy it will roll
the grass flat.

hedgehog

A hedgehog is a small animal. It has
prickles all over its back. When a
hedgehog is frightened, it rolls
itself up into a ball.

H h

heel

Your heel is the rounded part at the back of your foot below your ankle. It is also part of a shoe. This shoe has a high heel.

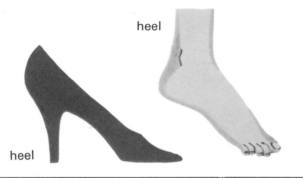

heel

heel

hill

A hill is a raised part of the earth. It is not as big as a mountain.

hide

When we hide we keep out of sight. Can you see David? He is hiding behind the bush.

hole

A hole is a gap in something solid.

helicopter

A flying machine that can go straight up in the air. Its blades lift it up into the air by going round and round.

high

High means far up. One kite is high up, but the others are low down.

holiday

When we have a holiday, we do not have to go to work or go to school.

hood

A hood is a covering for the head and neck. Jane's raincoat has a hood. The hood keeps her hair dry when it rains.

hook

A hook is a piece of metal which is bent so that it can hold things. You can hang your coat on a hook. A hook can be used to catch a fish.

horse

A horse is an animal. Sometimes horses are used to pull carts and sometimes people ride on them.

hospital

A hospital is a place where people stay if they are sick or hurt. Doctors and nurses work in hospitals.

H h

hotel

An hotel is a large building where travellers can get a meal and stay for the night.

hundred

Ten lots of ten make one hundred. This book has more than one hundred pages.

$$\blacksquare + \blacksquare + \blacksquare + \blacksquare + \blacksquare + \blacksquare + \blacksquare + \blacksquare + \blacksquare + \blacksquare = 100$$

hungry

When we feel hungry we want our food. We sometimes feel hungry if our dinner is late or we have missed a meal.

hunt

If we hunt for something it means we are looking for it. It also means to chase an animal.

hurt

When we are hurt we feel pain. Stings, cuts and bumps can all hurt.

ow see if you can spot all the things in this
icture beginning with the letter h and match
hem with their names at the bottom of the page.

hese are the things beginning with the letter h.

hair	handle	horse	hook
handkerchief	hat	hedgehog	helicopter

i

ice

When it is very cold, water freezes and becomes ice. The water in the pond has turned to ice and people are skating on it.

indoors

When we go indoors we go inside a building. Mary is going indoors because it is raining.

igloo

An igloo is an Eskimo's house. Igloos are usually made of blocks of snow and ice.

Indian

An Indian is a person who comes from India. There are also Indians in North America. North American Indians are called Red Indians

infant

An infant is a very young child. This baby is an infant.

information

Information is all the things we are told. This book informs you about the meanings of words.

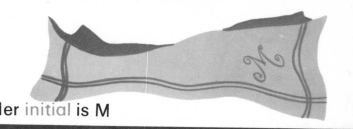

initial

Initial means first or beginning. An initial is also the letter with which a word begins. This handkerchief has Mary's initial on it. Her initial is M

ink

Ink is the liquid we use with a pen for writing or printing. Susan is filling her pen with ink.

insect

An insect is a small animal with six legs. The body of an insect is divided into three parts. Flies, bees, wasps and butterflies are insects.

I i

instrument

An instrument is a tool which helps us to do a job. A pen is an instrument we use when writing. Here are some other instruments.

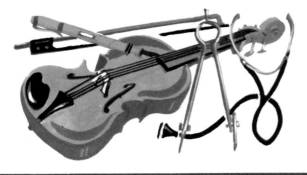

inventor

An inventor is a person who makes something new. This is Tim's invention. There has never been anything like it in the world before.

invisible

This is a picture of an invisible man. He cannot be seen.

invitation

You invite someone when you ask them to come to a party. Sue is writing the invitations for her party. She has invited lots of friends

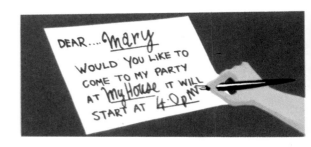

iron

Iron is a hard metal. An iron is also the instrument Mummy uses to get the creases out of our clothes.

island

An island is a piece of land with water all round it. Britain is an island.

Now see if you can spot all the things in this picture beginning with the letter i and match them with their names at the bottom of the page.

These are the things beginning with the letter i.

ice cream	island	iron
igloo	invitation card	Indian

j

a	b	c	d	e	f	g	h	i	j	k	l	m	n	o	p	q	r	s	t	u	v	w	x	y
A	B	C	D	E	F	G	H	I	J	K	L	M	N	O	P	Q	R	S	T	U	V	W	X	Y

jacket

A jacket is a short coat. Joan is wearing a long green coat but Susan is wearing a jacket.

jam

Jam is made by cooking fruit and sugar. Jane spreads jam on her bread.

When things are packed

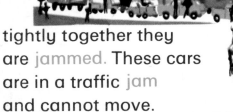

tightly together they are jammed. These cars are in a traffic jam and cannot move.

jelly

Jelly is nice to eat when it sets firm. It can also be a sort of jam.

jagged

Something which is jagged has an uneven edge. John hurt his leg on a jagged rock.

January

January is the first month of the year. New Year's day is on 1st January.

jewel

A jewel is a precious stone. A diamond is a jewel. In this piece of jewellery there are bits of diamond.

job

A job is a piece of work or a thing to do. Bob has a job as a paper boy. His job is to deliver the newspapers.

join

When we join two things we fasten them together. The sailors have joined the two pieces of rope together to make a long one.

Can you see the join?

joke

A joke is something said or done which makes us laugh. Jim played a joke on his friend on April Fool's Day.

journey

A journey is a trip or a visit. The longest journey so far has been the astronauts' trip to the moon.

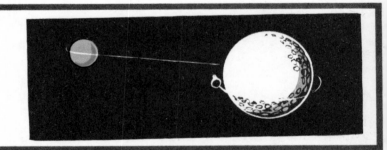

jug

A jug holds liquids. Mummy is holding this jug by the handle and pouring milk out of the spout. There are lots of different jugs.

This is a Toby jug.

J j

juice

Juice is the liquid part of fruit or vegetables. Most children have had orange juice. Have you ever tasted tomato juice?

July

July is the seventh month of the year. There are 31 days in July. Americans celebrate their independence on 4th July.

jumper

A person who leaps into the air is called a jumper. Sally is also wearing a jumper. It keeps her warm.

June

June is the sixth month of the year. There are 30 days in June. The longest day of the year is in June.

jungle

A jungle is a tangled mass of trees and vines. Wild animals live in the jungle.

junk

Junk is the old things people do not really want. It is also a type of Chinese sailing boat.

Now see if you can spot all the things in this picture beginning with the letter j and match them with their names at the bottom of the page.

These are the things beginning with the letter j.

jacket   jelly   juice   jungle
jug   junk   jumper   jam

k

a	b	c	d	e	f	g	h	i	j	k	l	m	n	o	p	q	r	s	t	u	v	w	x	y	z
A	B	C	D	E	F	G	H	I	J	K	L	M	N	O	P	Q	R	S	T	U	V	W	X	Y	

kangaroo

A kangaroo is an animal that lives in Australia. Kangaroos can jump long distances. The mother kangaroo carries her baby in a pocket or pouch at the front of her body.

kennel

A kennel is a dog's house. Bob's dog is asleep in his kennel. What is the name of Bob's dog?

kerb

The kerb is the edge of the pavement. Jill stands on the kerb. She is doing her kerb drill. She is looking out for traffic.

kettle

Mummy heats water in the kettle. When the water in the kettle boils, she makes the tea.

key

A key is a small piece of metal shaped to fit into the keyhole and turn the lock. Pianos and typewriters also have keys.

kick

When you kick something, you hit it with your foot. Tim kicks the football. He is a good kicker.

kind

When you are kind you are good to others. Jane is kind. She helps with the washing up.

Kind also means sort or type. What kind of boat is this?

kite

There are two kinds of kites. Tim is flying a kite. The other kite is a bird.

kitchen

A kitchen is a room where food is cooked and got ready.

K k

kitten

A kitten is a young cat. This kitten is playing with a ball of wool.

knife

We use a knife to cut things. Here are some different kinds of knives.

knot

When we tie some things together we knot them. There are different sorts of knots we can use.

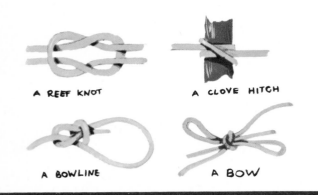

A REEF KNOT

A CLOVE HITCH

A BOWLINE

A BOW

knee

The knee is the joint in the middle of your leg. When we go down on our knees we are kneeling.

knock

When we knock something we hit it or bang on it. The postman is knocking at the door. Has the door got a knocker?

ow see if you can spot all the things in this
cture beginning with the letter k and match
em with their names at the bottom of the page.

ese are the things beginning with the letter k.

| kangaroo | kettle | kite | kitten |
| knife | key | kennel | knee |

a	b	c	d	e	f	g	h	i	j	k	l	m	n	o	p	q	r	s	t	u	v	w	x	y
A	B	C	D	E	F	G	H	I	J	K	L	M	N	O	P	Q	R	S	T	U	V	W	X	Y

l

label

If the label comes off the tin, we will not know what is inside it.

There are labels on all these tins.

There is a label on the inside of this jacket.

There are labels on this suitcase.

ladder

John is not tall enough to reach the apples at the top of the tree. He is climbing up a ladder so that he can pick the apples.

lake

A lake is water with land all round it. A lake is bigger than a pond.

Island

lamb

A lamb is a young sheep. How many lambs can you see in this picture?

lamp

A lamp gives us light. There is a street lamp outside this house. There is also a lamp over the front door.

land

Land is part of the surface of the Earth. About one third of the Earth is land. Two thirds are seas and oceans.

large

Large means very big. Mice are little but elephants are large.

last

Something which is last comes at the end. Tom is taking the last jam tart off the plate.

The tarts will not last until tea-time.

laugh

A laugh is a sound we make when we are happy. They laughed when they heard the funny joke.

laundry

A laundry is a place where clothes are washed. Clothes ready for washing are also called laundry.

L l

lazy

Someone who is lazy does not want to work. This lazy boy is not helping his friends to paint the boat. He is lazing in the sun.

leaf

A leaf is part of a tree or plant. There are also some other kinds of leaves.

The leaf of a tree

Tea leaves

The leaves of a book

leather

Leather is a material made from the skins of animals. Shoes, handbags and suitcases are sometimes made of leather.

left

These words are on the left side of the page. The picture is on the right of the words.

Left also means to go away. Tom left school at four o'clock today. He left his homework behind.

length

Length is how long a thing is. What is the length of this ruler?

inches

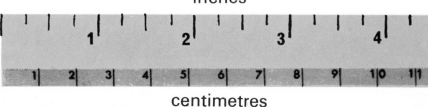

centimetres

letter

There are two sorts of letters. There are the letters of the alphabet and letters to be posted.

level

Level means flat and even. The table is level. Each leg is the same height.

library

A library is a place where many books are kept. Jack borrows books from the library in the town where he lives.

lighthouse

A lighthouse is a tower built in the sea or on the coast. There is a flashing light at the top of a lighthouse to guide the ships and warn them of danger.

lion

A lion is a large, fierce animal of the cat family. Lions live in Asia and Africa. You can see a lion at the zoo.

L l

liquid

A liquid is something which is not solid. Liquids flow easily. Water and milk are liquids.

list

A list is a lot of things written down. Mummy writes out a shopping list to remind her of what she wants to buy.

This is Peter's list for Father Christmas.

lonely

Lonely means being by yourself and not liking it. Robinson Crusoe was lonely.

lorry

Can you see the red lorry on this road? Lorries are used to carry heavy goods all over the country.

loud

Loud means noisy. Mother told Simon not to bang his drum so loudly because she had a headache.

luggage

Luggage is suitcases and bags. We take our luggage when we go on a journey.

Now see if you can spot all the things in this picture beginning with the letter l and match them with their names at the bottom of the page.

These are the things beginning with the letter l.

| lighthouse | lion | lorry | laundry list |
| ladder | lamp | lamb | leaf |

m

a	b	c	d	e	f	g	h	i	j	k	l	m	n	o	p	q	r	s	t	u	v	w	x	y
A	B	C	D	E	F	G	H	I	J	K	L	M	N	O	P	Q	R	S	T	U	V	W	X	Y

machine

A machine is something which can do things for us. Here are some machines that help us.

man

A boy grows up into a man. Here are two men and a boy.

many

Many means when there are a great number of things. Many children go to the cinema on Saturday mornings.

map

A map is a drawing showing all or part of the earth. Here is the pirates' map. Where is the hidden treasure?

March

March is the third month of the year. Sometimes it is very windy in March. Also, to march means to walk in step like soldiers.

marry

When a man and a woman marry
they become husband and wife.
At this marriage service, the
bride and bridegroom
are getting married.

match

Daddy lights
his pipe
with a match.

A match can
also be a
game between
two teams.

Match also means
when things are
alike. The ribbon
matches her dress.

material

Material is what a thing is
made of. Jane is buying
material to make a dress.

May

May is the fifth month of the
year. May Day is on the first of
May. Some people celebrate
May Day by dancing
round a maypole.

M m

meal

A meal is an amount of food which is eaten at one time. Most people eat three meals a day. Breakfast, dinner and tea are meals.

These are different sorts of meals.

measure

When we measure something, we find out the size of it. Daddy measures the length of Mick. He is measuring from his nose to the tip of his tail.

meat

Meat is the flesh of animals used for food. We can buy meat at the butcher's shop.

chop   joint   chicken

medicine

When we are ill, we sometimes take medicine to make us better again. Medicines may be tablets, powder, pills or liquids.

melt

Things melt when they change from being solid to liquid.

When the sun came out, the snowman melted.

mend

When we mend something, we repair it so it can be used again.

metal

There are many sorts of metal. Gold, silver, copper and lead are the names of metals. A metal is a mineral found under the ground.

milk

Milk is a white liquid which is good for us to drink. Cows give us milk. Some animals make milk for their young.

modern

Modern means of the present time. This building will be modern when it is finished.

money

Metals like gold, silver and copper can be made into coins. The coins are called money and you change them for things you want to buy.

We also use money which is made of paper.

month

We divide the year into twelve months. The names of the months are . . .

JANUARY FEBRUARY MARCH APRIL MAY JUNE
JULY AUGUST SEPTEMBER OCTOBER NOVEMBER DECEMBER

M m

motor

A motor is an engine which makes a thing go. A motor boat is driven by a motor.
A motorist is a person who drives a motor car.

mountain

A mountain is a very high hill. Some mountains have snow on top of them.

mouse

A mouse is a small animal that lives in fields, woods, barns or houses.

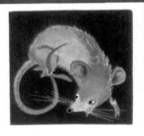

Mr. and Mrs.

When we talk or write to married people, we call them Mr and Mrs This envelope is addressed to Mr and Mrs Jones.

mug

A mug is a tall cup with a handle. Jane is drinking milk out of her mug.

music.

Music is the sound made by singing voices or musical instruments.

ow see if you can spot all the things in this
icture beginning with the letter m and match
hem with their names at the bottom of the page.

hese are the things beginning with the letter m.

| meat | mouse | money | mug |
| mountain | meal | motorist | medicine |

n

a	b	c	d	e	f	g	h	i	j	k	l	m	n	o	p	q	r	s	t	u	v	w	x	y
A	B	C	D	E	F	G	H	I	J	K	L	M	N	O	P	Q	R	S	T	U	V	W	X	Y

nail

A nail is a piece of pointed metal which is hammered in to join two things together. Nails are also the hard parts at the ends of your fingers and toes.

name

A name is the word by which a person or thing is known. This girl's name is Nancy. Her dog is named Fido.

narrow

Something which is narrow is not wide. The blue ribbon is narrower than the red one.

navy

A navy is a collection of ships and sailors belonging to one country. Bob is a sailor. He serves in the British Navy.

nature

Nature is all the things in the world not made by man. People who are interested in nature study learn about animals, plants and trees.

neck

Your neck joins your head to your body. Mary wears a necklace around her neck.

needle

Mummy uses a needle to do the sewing. She threads the cotton through the eye of the needle.

Mummy uses different kinds of needles to do the knitting.

neighbour

The people who live in this house have no neighbours on one side.

Mr Smith, the butcher, is their next door neighbour on the other side.

nest

A nest is a bird's home. Birds lay their eggs in nests.

How many baby birds can you see in the nest?

net

A net is used to catch things or to keep them in place. Net is also a type of dress material.

Fishing net

Mother's hairnet

new

Something which has been made but never worn or used very much is called new.

Daddy sold his old motor car. He bought a new one.

N n

newspaper

We read the newspaper to find out what has been happening in the world. It tells us the news. Daddy buys a newspaper every day.

next

Next means the one nearest. Jane sits next to Susan in class. They are neighbours.

Next Saturday they are going swimming together.

night

Night is the time from when the sun sets to when the sun comes up again.

It is dark at night but you might be able to see by the light of the moon.

nine

Nine is a number. If you add ten to nine, you get nineteen. Nine times ten is ninety.

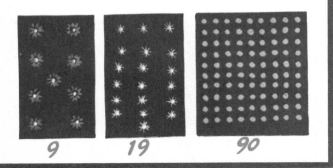

9   19   90

nobody

Nobody means no person or no one. Everyone was on time for school today, so nobody was late.

noise

A noise is a sound. John and his friends were playing a noisy game. They were making a lot of noise.

noon

Noon is twelve o'clock in the daytime. The children have their mid-day meal at noon.

Some children call this lunch and some children call this meal dinner.

north

The north is a direction. This aeroplane is flying north

notice

A notice is a printed or written message which gives us information. There is a notice on the tree about the school Sports Day.

Has John noticed it?

nought

Nought means there are no numbers. We write a figure nought like this — 0.

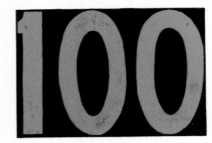

There are two noughts in one hundred.

November

November is the eleventh month of the year. Guy Fawkes Day is on 5th November.

N n

number

Number means how many of anything. The number of sheep in the field is six.

1, 2, 3, 4, 5, 6, 7, 8 and 9 are all numbers.

nurse

A nurse knows how to look after people who are sick or hurt.

This man and this woman are both nurses.

nut

A nut is a dry fruit or seed. It usually has a hard shell. An acorn is a nut and comes from the oak tree.

A nut is also a piece of metal which fits on to a bolt.

nylon

Nylon is a very strong material. Many of our clothes are made of nylon. Mummy's stockings are made of nylon.

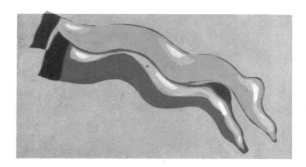

ow see if you can spot all the things in this
cture beginning with the letter n and match
em with their names at the bottom of the page.

ese are the things beginning with the letter n.

| notice | nut | nurse | newspaper |
| net | nail | needle | nest |

O

a	b	c	d	e	f	g	h	i	j	k	l	m	n	o	p	q	r	s	t	u	v	w	x	y
A	B	C	D	E	F	G	H	I	J	K	L	M	N	O	P	Q	R	S	T	U	V	W	X	Y

oak

An oak is a type of tree which has very hard wood.

ocean

An ocean is a big sea. There are five oceans in the world, the Atlantic, the Pacific, the Indian, the Arctic and the Antarctic.

October

October is the tenth month of the year. There are 31 days in October.

This calendar is open at the month of October.

off

The rider fell off his horse. He hopes the horse will not go off and leave him.

office

An office is a place where a business is carried on. Jane has a job in an office. She is a typist.

Does your father work in an office?

oil

Oil is a greasy or fat liquid.

Some oils are used to burn in lamps.

Some oils are used to make machines run smoothly.

old

People or things which are old have lived or been made for a long time.

Grandfather is an

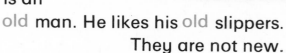

old man. He likes his old slippers. They are not new.

one

One is a number.

In this tank there is one goldfish and only one.

open

Open means not shut. The window is open. It has not been closed.

The cat has jumped through the opening.

opposite

These girls are facing each other. They are opposite to each other.

Opposite also means as different as possible. Fat is the opposite of thin.

O o

orange

An orange is a fruit. Jane is peeling an orange. She likes to eat oranges. Orange is also a colour. Jane's jumper is orange.

orchestra

An orchestra is a number of people playing musical instruments together.

ordinary

A thing is ordinary if it is very common. One hat is ordinary and the other hat is extra-ordinary.

own

To own is to have something. Oliver has his own bedroom. He owns lots of toys.

orchard

An orchard is ground where fruit trees grow. There are a lot of apple trees in this orchard.

out

The dog is coming out of the kennel. He has left his bone outside. It is raining outdoors.

ow see if you can spot all the things in this
cture beginning with the letter o and match
em with their names at the bottom of the page.

ese are the things beginning with the letter o.

oil   orchard
                                              orange
office   oak
                                              orchestra

p

a	b	c	d	e	f	g	h	i	j	k	l	m	n	o	p	q	r	s	t	u	v	w	x	y
A	B	C	D	E	F	G	H	I	J	K	L	M	N	O	P	Q	R	S	T	U	V	W	X	Y

pair

A pair is two things that go together. Mary has a pair of shoes and a pair of gloves.

paper

We can write or print or draw on paper. The pages of this book are made of paper. Other types of paper are wallpaper, wrapping paper and newspaper.

parachute

When a parachute opens it looks like an umbrella. People use parachutes to float down to earth from aeroplanes.

parent

A parent is a mother or a father. Susan's parents are taking her to the circus.

part

A part is a piece of something.
The boy left
part of the
cake to
eat later.

A centaur
was part man
and part horse.

path

A path is a way
for people or animals
to go. It is too
narrow for a car or a cart.

pedal

The pedal is the part on
which the foot is placed to
work a machine. When the
boy pedals, the bicycle moves.

passenger

A passenger is someone who
travels in a train, car, bus,
boat or aeroplane.
The passengers are getting
off the aeroplane.

pen

We use a
pen to
write with.

Pen is also the name of a
place for keeping animals.

P p

pencil

This boy is using a pencil to draw a picture. He will colour it with his coloured pencils.

people

People are human beings. Men, women, and children are people. How many people can you see in this picture?

pet

A pet is an animal which we keep at home. Dogs, cats, hamsters, birds and goldfish are often kept as pets. Do you own a pet?

petrol

Petrol is a liquid put into cars to make them go. It is kept in petrol pumps. The man is filling the petrol tank.

piano

A piano is a musical instrument. When we strike the keys on a piano, small hammers hit wires which give out musical sounds.

picnic

When we go on a picnic we eat out of doors.

Here is a family having a picnic on the beach.

pirate

A pirate is a sailor who robs ships at sea. This is the pirate flag. It is called the Skull and Crossbones.

Captain Morgan was a famous pirate.

plain

Something which is plain is ordinary and simple. Mother made a plain cake. It had no icing or cream.

A plain is also a piece of flat land.

plant

A plant is a tree, shrub, flower or vegetable. Here are some different plants.

Rose bush

Potted plants

P p

pond

A pond is a pool of water.
It is smaller than a lake. There are
ducks on the village pond.

port

A port is a place where ships
and boats can unload or shelter
from the storms at sea. Where
the ships tie up or anchor is
called the harbour.

The portside of a ship is the
left side of the ship when
you are looking forward.
The starboard side is on
the right side of the ship.

pump

A pump is used for
pushing liquid, air or
gas into or out of
things. This is a bicycle pump.

pupil

A pupil is someone
who is learning. It is
also the black part in
the centre of the eye.

puppet

A puppet is a doll
made to move by
strings or by
a person's hand.

puzzle

A puzzle is something
which is difficult to do
or understand. This is
a piece of a jig-saw puzzle.

Now see if you can spot all the things in this picture beginning with the letter p and match them with their names at the bottom of the page.

These are the things beginning with the letter p.

| puppet | piano | pencil |
| paper | parachute | pen |

q

a	b	c	d	e	f	g	h	i	j	k	l	m	n	o	p	q	r	s	t	u	v	w	x	y
A	B	C	D	E	F	G	H	I	J	K	L	M	N	O	P	Q	R	S	T	U	V	W	X	Y

quadrangle

A quadrangle is a four-sided shape. Squares or rectangles are quadrangles. We call a courtyard with four sides a quadrangle.

square

rectangle

quarter

A quarter is one of four equal parts. This cake has been cut into quarters.

quarrel

When we quarrel we argue and get angry. It is a fight with words.

queen

A queen is a woman ruler or the wife of a king. We also have Beauty Queens and Queen of the May.

question

We can ask a question if we want to find out something. The boy is asking the price of the car.

quick

Quick means fast. The dog ran so quickly that John could not catch him.

quiet

To be quiet is not to make a noise. People in hospital need their sleep. They cannot sleep if it is noisy.

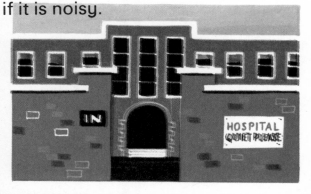

quilt

A quilt is a padded covering put on a bed to keep us warm. This is a patchwork quilt.

ow see if you can spot all the things in this cture beginning with the letter q and match em with their names at the bottom of the page.

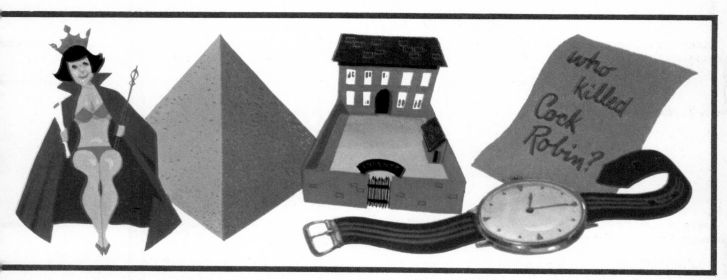

hese are the things beginning with the letter q.

queen   question   quadrangle

r

a	b	c	d	e	f	g	h	i	j	k	l	m	n	o	p	q	r	s	t	u	v	w	x	y
A	B	C	D	E	F	G	H	I	J	K	L	M	N	O	P	Q	R	S	T	U	V	W	X	Y

rabbit

A rabbit is a small animal with soft fur, long ears and a short tail. Have you ever seen a rabbit?

race

People race to see who is fastest. There are running races, car races and horse races. What type of race is in this picture?

radio

Radio is a way of sending and receiving words or music across space without using wires.

Some radios work from an electric plug.

Transistor radios do not have to be plugged in. They work off batteries.

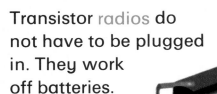

rain

Rain is water which falls from the clouds. We wear raincoats to keep us dry in the rain. It is raining hard.

rainbow

When the sun shines through the rain we can sometimes see a rainbow. It is an arch of seven colours in the sky.

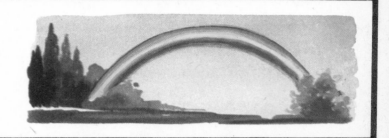

rake

A rake is a useful gardening tool. You can use it to gather up leaves or to level the ground.

rattle

A rattle is a toy which makes a noise when it is shaken. Baby has a rattle. When we rattle something we shake it so that it makes a noise.

reach

When you reach for something you are trying to get it. The baby is reaching for the mug.
Billy hopes to reach school on time.

real

Real means it is not a toy. It is the actual thing. Billy has a toy motor car but his father has a real one.

R r

record

There are several types of record. You can play a record and listen to it.

It was a record jump. It was the highest ever.

red

Red is a colour. All these things are red.

refrigerator

A refrigerator is something that keeps things cool. It can keep food fresh.

The butcher has a refrigerator room for his meat.

rescue

When we rescue someone, we save them from danger. Three sailors were rescued from the sea. They were saved from drowning.

rich

A rich person has a lot of money. A rich person may own a lot of things.

What would you buy if you were rich?

right

Right is the opposite of left
We have a right hand
and a left hand.

LEFT

RIGHT

Right also means
correct. Billy got
all the
sums right.

ring

A ring is something which is
shaped like a circle. Mother wears
a wedding ring which fits on
her finger.

A ring is also the sound of a
bell. Who is ringing the doorbell?

A ring.

Dancing
in a
ring.

river

A river is a large stream of
water which flows to the sea.

road

A road is a way on which cars
and people can travel
from place to place.

R r

rock

One type of rock is a big stone. You can also eat a stick of rock.

rocket

Rocket is the name of a firework or a machine that shoots up into the air.

root

A root is the part of a plant which grows downwards into the ground. It holds the plant in place.

rough

Rough things are not smooth. The road is rough. The cart bumps along it. The road needs to be made up.

row

When we arrange things in a row, we put them in a line. If we use oars in a boat we say that we row.

rust

Rust is the reddish brown crust that forms on iron when it gets wet. Here is a rusty nail.

ow see if you can spot all the things in this
icture beginning with the letter r and match
em with their names at the bottom of the page.

ese are the things beginning with the letter r.

rake	radio	rocket	ring
root	refrigerator	rain	rattle

S

a	b	c	d	e	f	g	h	i	j	k	l	m	n	o	p	q	r	s	t	u	v	w	x	y
A	B	C	D	E	F	G	H	I	J	K	L	M	N	O	P	Q	R	S	T	U	V	W	X	Y

safe

Safe means there is no danger. It is safer to cross the road on a crossing. A safe is also a very strong box for keeping valuable things safely.

sandwich

A sandwich is two slices of bread with cheese, ham or some other food between them. Mummy is giving the children sandwiches with egg and tomato filling.

saw

A saw is a tool for cutting. Daddy sawed the tree into logs with a circular saw. There are different types of saws.

HAND SAW

FRET-SAW

TENON SAW

scissors

Scissors are used for cutting paper or material. They have two blades. There are different types of scissors.

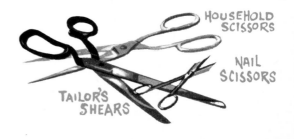

HOUSEHOLD SCISSORS

NAIL SCISSORS

TAILOR'S SHEARS

sea

The sea is the salt water that covers nearly three quarters of the world. When we go to the seaside we see the sea.

seed

A seed is the thing from which things grow. This sunflower grew from a seed.

September

September is the ninth month of the year

seven

Seven is a number. There are seven days in a week. If you add ten to seven it is seventeen. Ten times seven is seventy.

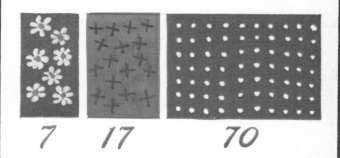

shadow

You cast a shadow when you get in front of the light. Have you ever tried to make shadow animals?

ship

A ship is a big boat which sails the sea. There are steam ships and sailing ships.

S s

shop

A shop is a place where you go to
buy things. This shop sells lots
of sweets. Which sweets
would you choose?

short

Short means not long or not tall.
Peter is shorter than Tom.
Bill is shorter than Peter.
Bill is the shortest.

Bill   Peter   Tom

side

The ship has portholes
or windows along its sides.
The boy is inside.
The captain
is outside.

six

Six is a number.
If you add ten to six, you get sixteen.
Ten times six is sixty.

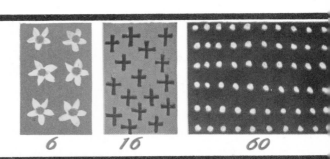

6   16   60

small

Small things are not big.
They are tiny or little.
A mouse is small. The button
is smaller. The ladybird is
the smallest of these three.

snow

It falls from the sky as soft
white flakes.
The snowman will not melt while
it is cold. The boys have knocked
his hat off with a snowball.

some

Some means a
number or amount
of. Here is a list
of some words.

soup

Soup is a liquid
food made by boiling
meat or vegetables. Have you
ever tasted kangaroo tail soup?

south

South is a
direction. The
aeroplane is flying
to the south.

spot

A spot is a place
or mark. Also to
spot something means to
notice it. Tom is train spotting.

stocking

A stocking is a
covering for the leg
and foot. Mummy
wears nylon stockings.

S s

stop

When something stops it finishes or comes to a standstill.
The car stops at the red traffic light.

straight

If it is straight it is not curved or bent. The man is painting a straight line down the middle of the road.

submarine

A submarine is a boat that travels under the water.

sweet

Sweet things taste like sugar or honey does. Cakes are sweet but lemons are sour.
Here is a tray of sweet things.

ow see if you can spot all the things in this
cture beginning with the letter s and match
em with their names at the bottom of the page.

ese are the things beginning with the letter s.

submarine	sandwich	scissors	shadow
snow	saw	sea	ship

t

a	b	c	d	e	f	g	h	i	j	k	l	m	n	o	p	q	r	s	t	u	v	w	x	y
A	B	C	D	E	F	G	H	I	J	K	L	M	N	O	P	Q	R	S	T	U	V	W	X	Y

tall

The factory chimney is tall.
The blocks of flats are taller.
The giant is the tallest but
he is not real.

teacher

A teacher is
anyone who helps
us learn. The man
is being taught to drive.

telephone

We use the telephone
to send messages
over wires to
another place.

ten

Ten is a number.
You have ten
toes altogether.
Two tens are twenty.

tea

Tea is a hot drink which is
made from the dried leaves of
the tea plant.

Tea is also the meal we have
during the afternoon.

television

Television is a means
of sending pictures
through space. We
need an aerial as well as a set.

tent

A tent is a shelter
that can be moved
from place to place. Tents are
made of material, poles and ropes.

thank

When we thank someone, we tell them that they have pleased us. Mary thanked her aunt for the present.

She said, "Thank you".

thick

Thick is the opposite of thin. This tree has a thick trunk. It is very wide.

The other tree is thin.

three

Three is a number. If you add ten to three you get thirteen. Three times ten is thirty.

3   13   30

tie

When we tie something we fasten it. John ties his shoelace. Men and boys wear ties round their necks. John has a red tie.

tool

A tool is anything we use for doing work. We need a saw to cut wood, a hammer to nail things and a shovel to dig with.

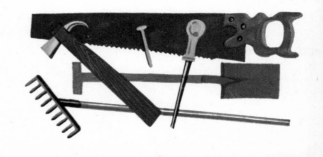

T t

town

A town is a place where people live. It is smaller than a city. There are many houses and shops in towns.

Do you live in a town?

tractor

A tractor is a machine used on a farm. It can pull farm machinery.

traffic

Traffic is the people and the cars moving along a street or a road.

tunnel

A tunnel is an underground way. Trains sometimes go through tunnels.

toy

A toy is anything we use for playing. Jane had a lot of toys at Christmas. Her favourite toy is a doll.

truck

A truck is a big open wagon or cart for carrying heavy loads.

two

Two is a number. You have two hands, two feet, two eyes and two ears. This is the numeral two.

2

Now see if you can spot all the things in this picture beginning with the letter t and match them with their names at the bottom of the page.

These are the things beginning with the letter t.

telephone	tent	tractor	toy
three	television set	tie	truck

u

ugly

Ugly means not nice to look at.
The witch has an ugly face.
She lives in an ugly castle.

uncle

Your uncle is the brother of
your mother or father.
His wife is your aunt.

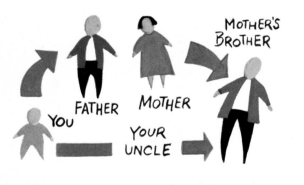

underwear

Underwear is what
we wear next to
the body.

umbrella

Sue is holding an umbrella over
her head as it is raining. The
umbrella helps to keep her dry.
Sunshades are umbrellas which
keep the sun off us.

under

Under means below.
Baby has dropped
her spoon under the
table. Bob climbs under to get it.

undo

To undo means
to unfasten. Jim
is undoing his
birthday present.

uniform

A uniform is the clothes that some people wear to tell us what jobs they do. Soldiers, nurses and policemen all wear uniforms.

SOLDIER SAILOR NURSE POLICEMAN POSTMAN

up

Up is the opposite of down.
The boy is going up.
He is going up to his bedroom.

upset

When we upset something, we tip it over. Mary upset the milk on her dress.

Upset also means to be worried about something. Jane was upset when she lost her purse.

U u

upside-down

When something is upside-down, its top is at the bottom. The bottle is upside-down so that the water drains out of it.

These words are upside down.

upstairs

Upstairs is on the floor above. Tim's bedroom is upstairs. He goes upstairs to bed.

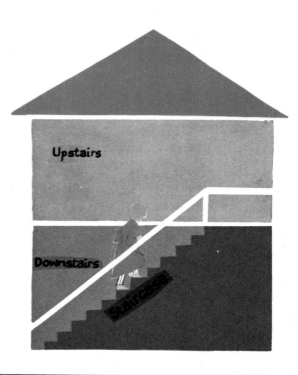

us

When we talk about us, we mean ourselves and other people. "Uncle has given us a present," said Jill to her sisters. The present was for all of them, not just Jill.

useful

Useful things are things that we find of help. Which of these things would be useful if you had to bake a cake?

ow see if you can spot all the things in this
cture beginning with the letter u and match
em with their names at the bottom of the page.

hese are the things beginning with the letter u.

umbrella   underwear   uniform

V

a	b	c	d	e	f	g	h	i	j	k	l	m	n	o	p	q	r	s	t	u	v	w	x	y
A	B	C	D	E	F	G	H	I	J	K	L	M	N	O	P	Q	R	S	T	U	V	W	X	Y

van

A van is a type of lorry. When they moved into a new house their furniture was sent to the new address in a furniture van.

vase

There is a vase on the table. Mummy is going to put some flowers in the vase. What colour is the vase?

vegetable

A vegetable is a plant grown for food. Potatoes, carrots and peas are vegetables.

village

A village is a place where people live. It is smaller than a town. Do you live in a village, a town or a city?

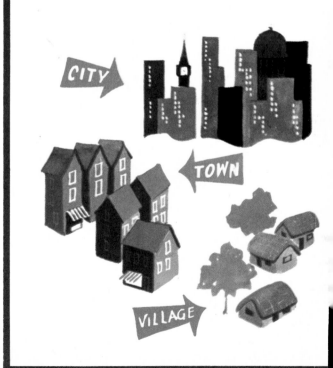

CITY

TOWN

VILLAGE

visitor

A visitor is someone who comes to see us. We can visit other people or places. Bill visited the rocket launching pad.

voice

The sound made through our mouths is called our voice. Some people have deep voices.

vowels

a, e, i, o, u are called vowels. Other letters are called consonants.

Vowels say their own names or short sounds as in the beginning of the names of these things in the picture.

Now see if you can spot all the things in this picture beginning with the letter v and match them with their names at the bottom of the page.

These are the things beginning with the letter v.

van   vase   vegetable   vowel

a	b	c	d	e	f	g	h	i	j	k	l	m	n	o	p	q	r	s	t	u	v	w	x	y
A	B	C	D	E	F	G	H	I	J	K	L	M	N	O	P	Q	R	S	T	U	V	W	X	Y

walk

When we walk we go forward by putting one foot in front of the other. Jim is taking his dog for a walk in the park.

They are both walking.

water

Water is a liquid. Rain is water. There is water in oceans, rivers and lakes. We drink water and use it for washing.

watch

To watch means to look at something. A wrist watch is also the small clock we wear on our wrists.

west

The west is a direction. The sun sets in the west. This aeroplane is flying to the west.

week

A week is seven days. Here are the names of the days of the week.

MONDAY
TUESDAY
WEDNESDAY
THURSDAY
FRIDAY
SATURDAY
SUNDAY

wheel

A wheel is a frame like a circle that turns round.
Wheels are made of wood or metal.

white

White is a colour. Snow is white.
The bride wore a white dress at
her wedding. Her shoes were white, too.

White is
the opposite
of black.

| white |
| black |

whole

When something is whole it is all there.
It is complete. This jig-saw puzzle is
not whole. One piece is missing.

wind

Wind is moving air.
The strong wind
blew Sue's
hat off.

To wind means to
tighten the spring
of a machine so that
it will go by itself.
Daddy winds the clock.

winter

Winter is one of the four seasons
of the year. It is the coldest season.
It snows sometimes. Most plants
rest during the winter.

 SPRING

 SUMMER

 AUTUMN

 WINTER

wish

When we wish for something, we want
it badly. We long for it.
Each boy is wishing for something
different. What are their wishes?

Ww

woman

A **woman** is a grown up girl.
Mummy is a **woman**. How many
women are there in this picture?

word

A **word** is a group of letters
that makes sense.
When we speak or write
we use **words**.

Which of these are **words**?

work

When we **work**, we make
an effort to do something.
Jim worked hard to finish
his **homework**.

Also when
something is
broken we
say it will
not **work**.

world

The **world** is the earth and
all the people who live on it.
The astronauts on the way to
the moon took
photographs of
the **world** from
out in space.

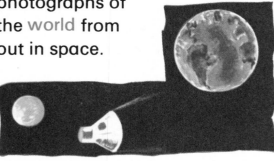

write

When we **write**, we make
letters and words. The teacher
writes on the blackboard. His
writing is very clear.

ow see if you can spot all the things in this
cture beginning with the letter w and match
em with their names at the bottom of the page.

ese are the things beginning with the letter w.

water	wheel	writing
watch	woman	world

X

a	b	c	d	e	f	g	h	i	j	k	l	m	n	o	p	q	r	s	t	u	v	w	x	y
A	B	C	D	E	F	G	H	I	J	K	L	M	N	O	P	Q	R	S	T	U	V	W	X	Y

X-ray

An X-ray is a photograph which a doctor takes of the inside of our body.

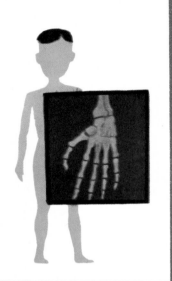

xylophone

A xylophone is a musical instrument. A xylophone is played by striking the keys with little wooden hammers.

y

a	b	c	d	e	f	g	h	i	j	k	l	m	n	o	p	q	r	s	t	u	v	w	x	y
A	B	C	D	E	F	G	H	I	J	K	L	M	N	O	P	Q	R	S	T	U	V	W	X	Y

yacht

A yacht is a small sailing ship or boat. The wind fills the sails and drives it through the water. Sometimes there are yacht races.

yarn

Yarn is spun thread. Mummy makes jumpers, gloves, and socks from yarn. A yarn is also a story. Travellers often tell yarns about their adventures.

ADVENTURE YARNS

YARN

year

There are 52 weeks in a year. There are twelve months in a year. There are four seasons in a year.

Jane is five years old. There is a candle for each year.

yellow

Yellow is a colour. Gold, butter, primroses and lemonade are yellow. All the things in this picture are yellow.

yelp

A yelp is the noise made by a dog when it is excited or when it is in pain. Bob's dog yelped when he accidentally trod on its tail.

young

Young is the opposite of old. It means not having lived very long.

Baby is young.

Puppies are young dogs.

Z

a	b	c	d	e	f	g	h	i	j	k	l	m	n	o	p	q	r	s	t	u	v	w	x	y

A	B	C	D	E	F	G	H	I	J	K	L	M	N	O	P	Q	R	S	T	U	V	W	X	Y

zebra

A zebra is an animal. Zebras look like horses but they have black and white stripes around their bodies.

Zebras are wild animals but you can see them at the zoo.

zero

Zero means nothing. We write zero as 0.

"Five, four, three, two, one, zero, blast off!"

zip-fastener

A zip-fastener is sometimes used to join two pieces of material together. There is a zip-fastener in this pencil case.

zig-zag

To zig-zag means to turn sharply from side to side. This path zig-zags across the garden.

zoo

A zoo is a place where wild animals are kept in cages or pens. Daddy took Simon to the zoo to see the animals.

Now see if you can spot all the things in this picture beginning with the letters x, y and z. Match them with their names at the bottom of the page.

These are the things beginning with the letters x, y and z.

yacht	yarn	zip-fastener
xylophone	zebra	yellow